UNDERSTANDING THE PARANORMAL

INVESTIGATING GHOSTS AND THE SPIRIT WORLD

SUSAN HENNEBERG

Britannica
Educational Publishing

IN ASSOCIATION WITH

ROSEN
EDUCATIONAL SERVICES

Published in 2015 by Britannica Educational Publishing (a trademark of Encyclopædia Britannica, Inc.) in association with The Rosen Publishing Group, Inc.
29 East 21st Street, New York, NY 10010

Distributed exclusively by Rosen Publishing.
To see additional Britannica Educational Publishing titles, go to rosenpublishing.com.

First Edition

Britannica Educational Publishing
J. E. Luebering: Director, Core Reference Group
Anthony L. Green: Editor, Compton's by Britannica

Rosen Publishing
Hope Lourie Killcoyne: Executive Editor
Christine Poolos: Editor
Nelson Sá: Art Director
Designer: Brian Garvey
Cindy Reiman: Photography Manager

Library of Congress Cataloging-in-Publication Data

Henneberg, Susan, author.
Investigating ghosts and the spirit world/Susan Henneberg.—First edition.
        pages cm.—(Understanding the paranormal)
Audience: Grades 5 to 8.
Includes bibliographical references and index.
ISBN 978-1-62275-863-0 (library bound) — ISBN 978-1-62275-865-4 (paperback) —
ISBN 978-1-62275-866-1 (6-pack)
1. Ghosts—Juvenile literature. 2. Parapsychology—Juvenile literature. I. Title.
BF1461.H45 2015
133.1—dc23

2014021039

Manufactured in the United States of America

Cover, p. 1 Tom Tom/Shutterstock.com; pp. 4-5 Print Collector/Hulton Fine Art Collection/Getty Images; p. 7 LOOK-foto/SuperStock; p. 8 Steve Russell/Toronto Star/Getty Images; p. 9 © North Wind Picture Archives/Alamy; p. 12 siouxsinner/Shutterstock.com; p. 13 © iStockphoto.com/Renphoto; pp. 16, 17 © Mary Evans Picture Library/Alamy; p. 18 Library of Congress Prints and Photographs Division; p. 19 Henk Paul/Shutterstock.com; p. 21 Danish Siddiqui/Reuters/Landov; p. 23 Archive Photos/Moviepix/Getty Images; p. 24 © Charles Walker/TopFoto/The Image Works; p. 26 Orlando Sentinel/McClatchy-Tribune/Getty Images; p. 29 © AP Images; p. 30 Science & Society Picture Library/Getty Images; p. 32 The British Library; p. 35 © Everett Collection; p. 36 Wendy Carlson/© Syfy/Courtesy Everett Collection; p. 38 © iStockphoto.com/ibusca; interior pages background images © iStockphoto.com/Kivilvim Pinar, © iStockphoto.com/mitja2.

CONTENTS

INTRODUCTIO

According to several recent surveys, belief i existence of ghosts is widespread—in fact, nearly half of all Americans believe that ghosts are real, a sentiment that is shared by a similar proportion of people living in Canada and the United Kingdom.

Many people believe that ghosts are the souls or spirits of those who have died, and places that are said to be haunted are often thought to be associated by a haunting spirit with some strong emotion of the past—remorse, fear, or the terror of a violent death. Of course, other people believe that ghosts exist only in our imaginations. Whatever you believe, ghost stories have been told for thousands of years, in almost every culture.

Paranormal investigators, popularly known as ghost hunters, look for proof that ghosts are real or for rational explanations for ghostly activity. Some use high-tech instruments to try to record the sounds of ghosts and take pictures of them. Sometimes these photos show shadowy shapes next to living people. Some of their videos show objects that appear to be moving by themselves.

Though most scientists are skeptical that ghosts exist, haunted houses, spooky stories, and ghost-hunting reality TV shows all reflect our continuing fascination with ghosts. There is a whole world of unexplained events ready to explore.

History, literature, and folklore are filled with stories about the appearances of ghosts and apparitions.

WHAT ARE GHOSTS?

It was just another night on the job for the staff of Everyday Paranormal. First, the ghost hunters set up their equipment. Then they spread out. On this night, they were investigating the Myrtles Plantation. This large mansion in Louisiana was built before the Civil War. Caretakers and visitors reported seeing ghosts. Some said they heard sounds of children crying. Some thought they felt hands tugging on their pants legs.

Nothing happened until 2:00 AM. Then ghost hunter Barry Klinge, waiting in the dark in the main house, felt a big drop in temperature. A cold spot moved over him. His instruments showed a drop of almost 40 degrees. He smelled cigar smoke and perfume. He was startled when a rock skittered across the floor and bumped into a wall. Brad Klinge, Barry's brother, waited in the old slave quarters on the

Ghost hunters believe that the Myrtles Plantation in Louisiana is one of the most haunted houses in America.

property. Brad suddenly felt a hard strike on his back. When he turned around, no one was there.

The team members of Everyday Paranormal first look for scientific explanations for the spooky events that happen during their investigations. Open windows can cause cold spots. Curtains can hold smells for decades. Voices can carry in the stillness of night. The Klinge brothers carefully reviewed the data they collected that night. They found that most of the events could not be explained. They deduced that there were ghosts at the Myrtles Plantation.

Paranormal investigators use talcum powder as a trap to capture evidence of ghostly footprints.

TYPES OF GHOSTS

People who believe in ghosts say that they are the souls of dead persons that appear in some form to the living. Many societies perform funeral rites to help souls travel to the afterlife so they will not return to haunt the living. Ghosts are considered to be "paranormal" beings. This means that they are outside the range of normal experience or scientific explanation.

For hundreds of years, believers and nonbelievers have debated whether or not ghosts exist. Those who think that all ghostly events can be explained by science are called skeptics.

According to descriptions or depictions provided by believers, there are several kinds of ghosts. A human-looking figure that can be seen is called an apparition. For instance, some visitors to the White House have seen a hazy Abraham Lincoln in the bedroom named after him. One such visitor was Queen

Apparitions are human-looking figures that appear to be dead people coming back to haunt the living.

Wilhelmina of the Netherlands. She was visiting President Franklin Delano Roosevelt in 1942. Reports say that she fainted after she answered a knock on the bedroom door. She said she saw Lincoln in his top hat and dark suit. According to ghost believers, apparitions most often haunt places to which they had strong emotional ties. These may be places where they lived, worked, or died.

Another type of ghost is a poltergeist. The word comes from two German words, *polter*, which means "noise," and *geist*, which means "spirit." Some people believe that poltergeists are mean troublemakers. They make loud noises, send objects flying off shelves,

BELIEFS ABOUT GHOSTS

A Huffington Post/YouGov poll conducted in 2012 showed that 45 percent of U.S. adults believe in ghosts or that the spirits of dead people can come back. In addition, 28 percent claimed they have seen or been in the presence of a ghost, and 43 percent said they don't think ghosts are harmful. Some experts think that believing in ghosts helps people to be less anxious about death.

or throw things. These events can range from mildly annoying to causing physical harm.

Some ghost experts believe that poltergeists appear to focus on one particular family member. Most often they target a youth going through puberty. This seemed to be the case in 1960 with a family in Baltimore, Ohio. Glass pitchers, a flowerpot, a sugar bowl, and drinking glasses flew off tables and shelves and shattered on the floor. Furniture was destroyed. Police officers investigated the house. They couldn't find anything that could cause the objects to move or explode. City engineers brought a seismograph to measure earthquakes. Plumbers and electricians were called. None of them could find causes. The destructive force didn't quit until the 17-year-old boy who lived in the house began to talk to a therapist about his problems.

Sometimes apparitions and poltergeist activities occur in the same place. According to writer Brad Steiger, in 1999 a ghost-hunting team was called to a Godfather's Pizza restaurant in Ogden, Utah. Ghostly figures appeared to staff and customers. A jukebox played music when the power to the building was shut off. Light bulbs flew across the room. The owner heard whistling in the kitchen when no one was there. The investigators looked into the history of the area. They found that the site had once been a pauper's field. This

OUIJA BOARDS

Some people believe they can communicate with ghosts using a Ouija board. The name "Ouija" comes from the words *oui* and *ja* which mean "yes" in French and German, respectively.

The Ouija board is an oblong piece of wood or cardboard with letters of the alphabet inscribed in a half-moon along the edge. A small heart-shaped board is placed on top of it. Participants each lightly place a finger on the small board, which spirits supposedly move around on the larger board. As it touches the letters it may spell out words or sentences.

Some ghost experts advise children against playing with a Ouija board. They warn that innocent players may be inviting dangerous ghosts to bring trouble to them. However, skeptics say it is a person's subconscious mind and not a ghost that is moving the small platform on the board.

The first Ouija board was introduced in 1890 as a harmless parlor game.

is an old cemetery where poor people were often buried in shallow, unmarked graves. Maybe, the team thought, the spirits wanted better burials.

COMMUNICATING WITH GHOSTS

Some people believe that a medium can make contact with spirits of the dead during a séance. *Séance* means

Séance participants hope to communicate with a loved one who has died.

"sitting" in French. It is a meeting of usually five to ten people who try to contact spirits. They sit in a circle and sometimes hold hands. A medium is a person who is supposedly able to go into a trance and act as the go-between for the spirits and the séance participants.

Sometimes the medium speaks for the spirit in a different voice. Other ways of communicating with spirits are through Ouija boards or automatic writing. Automatic writing occurs when the medium is directed by the spirit to write. Whether some people actually possess the ability to communicate with spirits, however, remains open to debate.

THE HISTORY OF GHOSTS

Imagine a life thousands of years ago without television, computers, or cell phones. There were no books, movies, or even electric lights. How did ancient people entertain themselves at night? They told stories huddled around fires to keep out the dark. They often told scary stories about things they couldn't explain. They wondered what happened when they died and told stories about that, too.

ANCIENT GHOST STORIES

Graves of our early ancestors showed that they believed in life after death. They would bury their dead with food, clothes, and weapons. Many cultures showed that they believed that people could return after death. Hieroglyphics created by ancient Egyptians tell about

ATHENODORUS CONFRONTS THE SPECTRE.

According to Pliny the Younger, Athenodorus was determined to figure out why his rented house was haunted by a ghost.

ghostlike figures that protected dead bodies. These ghosts needed offerings of food and drink or they would leave the body and haunt the living.

A historian of ancient Rome named Pliny the Younger penned one of the earliest known ghost stories around 100 CE. A man named Athenodorus rented a house. It was said to be haunted by an old man with chains around his hands. One night, the ghost appeared. It beckoned Athenodorus to follow it to a place outside in a courtyard. Then it vanished. The next day, Athenodorus dug up the spot. He found a human skeleton wrapped in chains. He gave the bones a proper burial. He never saw the ghost again. Helping a ghost move on to an afterlife is a common story in many cultures.

In the Middle Ages, legends were told of ghostly armies fighting battles at night in the forests. Later, Renaissance storytellers told tales of ghosts of murdered people coming back to haunt their murderers. English poet and dramatist William Shakespeare used some of these stories in his plays.

SPIRITUALISM

A new movement rose in the United States during the mid-1800s. It was called spiritualism. It began in Hydesville, New York, in the home of the Fox sisters. The Fox family had been disturbed by unexplained rapping on the walls at night. The youngest sister, Kate Fox, began to rap back. She developed a code of raps that allowed her to communicate with the supposed spirit, and the spirit was said to have identified himself as a man who had been murdered in the house. Kate and one of her

For a few years, the Fox sisters convinced many Americans that they could communicate with spirits using a code of raps.

older sisters, Maggie, soon became famous mediums. They gave séances all over the country. Other mediums attracted followers, and the movement spread to Europe. Thousands of people attended séances. They hoped to hear from dead friends and relatives.

HARRY HOUDINI

In his later years famed magician Harry Houdini campaigned against mind readers, mediums, and others who claimed supernatural powers. He argued that they were charlatans who produced all of their effects through natural means and various tricks. In 1924 he agreed to be on a panel of experts organized by *Scientific American* magazine. The editors promised $5,000 (about $67,000 today) to any medium proved to have real ability to contact spirits. Houdini attended a séance with famous medium Mina Crandon, who wanted to win the prize. He discovered she was using devices hidden under her feet to move objects in a room. Houdini and his wife, however, agreed to conduct an experiment in spiritualism: the first to die was to try to communicate with the survivor. His widow declared the experiment a failure before her death in 1943.

Mina Crandon poses with illusionist Harry Houdini (right) and other members of the board that investigated her séances.

The Fox sisters later admitted that they had lied. They created the rapping sounds by popping their finger and toe joints. Spiritualism began to die out as mediums faking their spirit contacts were exposed.

STORIES FROM OTHER CULTURES

Many cultures around the world have traditions of ghosts. The Dogon people of West Africa believe that spirits of the dead cause trouble in villages. The spirits do not want to leave. Young men perform a dance during which they wear masks of some part of life that the dead people might miss. The spirits see the masks and are

Dogon men wear colorful masks to convince the spirits of the dead to move to the next world.

ORIGINS OF HALLOWEEN

In many cultures there was a belief that the souls of the dead come back to visit their homes one day out of the year. Some souls wanted revenge on their enemies. People would sometimes wear masks and other disguises so that those souls would not recognize them. In Europe, these beliefs combined with a Catholic holy day called All Saints' Day; this is a day commemorating all the saints of the church, both known and unknown. The night before All Saints' Day became All Hallows' Eve, or Halloween.

able to say good-bye. They then are able to move peacefully to the next world.

Many people in Mexico celebrate the Día de los Muertos, or Day of the Dead. It is a time to remember loved ones who have died. Family members make favorite foods and set a place at the table for them. Toys and food are created in the shape of skulls or skeletons.

Japanese children are told stories about ghosts called the *yurei*. These are spirits of people who died suddenly or violently. Sometimes they represent a person who died after feeling powerful emotions such as revenge or jealousy. The *yurei* are said to look like young women with long black hair and dress in white.

Relatives help a young girl in India (right) exorcise her evil spirits during a ghost fair.

When their conflicts are resolved, they can travel to the afterlife and join their ancestors.

In some parts of rural India, many people believe that family members are possessed by spirits and ghosts. They are brought to the "ghost buster" fair in Malajpur to have the ghosts exorcised, or driven out of the suffering person. As many as 10,000 people arrive each year seeking help from temple priests.

SCIENTIFIC EXPLANATIONS OF GHOSTS

Many people don't think that ghosts exist. They believe that all unexplained events have a scientific cause. Some people who are curious about supernatural phenomena become paranormal investigators. The field of paranormal investigation has exploded. There are ghost detectives in just about every U.S. state.

Looking for ghosts became popular after the 1984 comedy film *Ghostbusters* was released. Real ghost investigators think this movie is a fun, but not very accurate, picture of what they do. Many paranormal investigators use rigorous scientific methods to track down sources of alleged ghostly activity. However, some of the ghost hunters on popular reality TV shows seem more interested in creepy special effects. They don't want to find a real, but unexciting, explanation for a spooky event.

The 1984 comedy film Ghostbusters *introduced audiences to the field of paranormal investigation.*

EARLY INVESTIGATIONS

Before the invention of the camera and sound recorder people could only tell stories about ghostly events. Early photographers quickly found ways to use their new equipment to feed society's interest in ghosts. One of the first "spirit photographers" was William Mumler. After the Civil War, he took a photo of Mary Todd Lincoln. She was the widow of President Abraham Lincoln. There

William H. Mumler, a spirit photographer, took photographs of people with the images of their dead loved ones in the background.

was a faint image of Lincoln standing behind her. Mumler was later accused of being a fraud.

Early photographs often show mysterious objects. These could be caused by poor camera skills or improper developing. For instance, double exposures in older cameras happen if the film doesn't advance after taking a picture. This can produce eerie figures that look transparent. Glowing orbs in a picture can be caused when a camera's flash reflects off dust in the air.

MODERN INVESTIGATIONS

Today, paranormal investigators visit haunted sites and conduct interviews with site owners and others who have experienced unexplained events. Investigators use special equipment, called paratechnology, to detect paranormal activity. One of these tools is an electromagnetic field (EMF) meter. Many areas have high EMF levels because of computers, cell phones, nearby power lines, or faulty wiring. Some investigators believe a sudden spike in EMF signals a ghost. They also use thermometers, Geiger counters, and motion detectors.

Paratechnology allows ghost detectives to see and hear things that are outside the levels of human senses. Some paranormal investigators think that ghosts are not able to show up in the range of the color spectrum the human eye can see but instead can be visible in the infrared (IR) part of the spectrum. This is the section

Ghost investigators use high-tech instruments such as EMF readers to detect electromagnetic fields said to be produced by ghosts.

that we detect only as heat. Investigators use digital video recorders (DVRs) with IR and heat imaging cameras. They also use electronic voice phenomenon (EVP) recorders. These devices record sounds below the level of human hearing.

After an investigation, ghost detectives examine the data they have collected and try to find explanations for what people at a site have experienced. Sometimes, however, they detect large changes in temperature and other phenomena that they can't explain. They will play

PRIZE AT STAKE

Magician James Randi established an organization in 1999 called the Committee for the Scientific Investigation of Claims of the Paranormal. He offers a prize of $1,000,000 to anyone who can show scientific evidence of paranormal activity. In 2008, an applicant wanted to show that he could pick up a ghost EVP at a grave site called the Devil's Chair in Florida. However, he had no way of proving that any voices heard were those of a ghost. As yet, no one has won the prize.

back the video and audio recordings. They may see apparitions and hear voices that they didn't see or hear when they were at the site.

THE REAL CAUSES OF HAUNTINGS, ACCORDING TO SCIENTISTS

Scientists believe they can explain why people think they have seen or heard a ghost or live in a haunted house. Some doctors say that sleepers can see visions in the state between sleeping and consciousness, called a waking dream. People can hallucinate if they accidently inhale carbon monoxide leaking from a stove or heater. Other chemicals that might produce visions include pesticides or formaldehyde, which can be found in furniture or carpets.

Some paranormal activity can be explained by normal events that people don't understand. Poltergeists might be blamed for moving furniture around or opening doors and windows. This movement might occur because a house is built on unstable ground. The foundation or soil under it contracts or expands with changes in temperature or moisture. This causes the house to shift. The movement can cause a clock to suddenly stop, items to fall from shelves, or chairs to cross a room. Small earthquakes can do the same things.

Other supposed hauntings can have natural sources. Noisy mice might be crawling in the walls of a house. A draft from a window or chimney can cause cold spots. Voices picked up by sound recorders can come from radio stations. Low frequency sound waves, known as infrasound, can cause people to think ghosts are present. The sound waves can cause people nearby to feel nervous, nauseous, or dizzy. In one case two ghost investigators found very low sound waves coming from an electric fan. Sound waves can vibrate the human eye. This can cause people to see things that are not there or that are blurry.

THE BROWN MOUNTAIN LIGHTS

Scientists have had to work hard to explain the Brown Mountain lights. These are bright globes in the mountains in North Carolina. According to Native American legend, the lights have been seen for hundreds of years. These mysterious glowing orbs have been investigated by the U.S. government, science museums, and private groups, and have been featured on popular TV programs such as *The X-Files*. One group thinks it has found the answer. Group members used Geiger counters, night vision cameras, EMF detectors, and long-range temperature gauges in their investigations. They concluded that the lights were naturally caused by the specific geology of the mountains.

Scientists investigating the Brown Mountain lights have set up cameras to capture the lights from several different viewpoints.

THE IGNIS-FATUUS, OR WILL-O'-THE-WISP.

Balls of light found in swampy areas are named after a wisp, which is a bundle of sticks sometimes used as a torch.

Mysterious lights found outdoors can have natural causes. Rotting plants in wet areas produce methane gas. Methane mixing with gases in the air can ignite. Sometimes these lights are called will-o'-the-wisps. In other cases, reflections from car headlights can look like ghostly orbs.

Most scientists are skeptical that ghosts exist. The equipment often used to detect ghosts is not made for that purpose. There is no proof that any data shows evidence of ghosts. People tend to believe supernatural causes for events they don't understand. Scientists are confident that all evidence of ghost activity will show natural, if sometimes complicated, causes.

GHOSTS IN LITERATURE AND POPULAR CULTURE

Ghosts have been popular characters in literature, film, and television. Many people enjoy the thrill of a scary story or a horror movie. They know, even when they are frightened, that they will be safe at the end. Other people are interested in life after death. They like finding out as much as they can about communicating with ghosts.

Children and adults have also enjoyed haunted house board games, video games, and smartphone and tablet applications. Some games can be frightening for the participants: Ghosts, zombies, and ghouls are unleashed into the world for game players to find and eliminate. Others provide the fun and adventure of solving spooky mysteries.

GHOSTS IN LITERATURE

Ghosts appeared in Elizabethan times as spirits of murdered characters. Two of William Shakespeare's plays have ghosts playing important roles. In *Hamlet*, a ghost of Hamlet's father appears in the first act. He announces that he has been murdered by his brother, Hamlet's uncle. In *Macbeth*, the ghost of the murdered hero Banquo appears only to Macbeth.

A ghost appears in an 1820 short story by Washington Irving called "The Legend of Sleepy Hollow," in which the ghost of a headless horseman chases a terrified schoolteacher through an eerie forest. Twenty year later, Charles Dickens, a British writer, published *A Christmas Carol*. In the story, the greedy Ebenezer Scrooge is visited by the ghosts of Christmas past, present, and future.

John Leech

Marley's Ghost.

Ghosts and haunted houses have been popular topics in poems, plays, short stories, and novels. Authors Edgar Allan Poe, Shirley Jackson, Stephen King, Toni Morrison, and Alice Sebold have made their readers nervous with ghostly characters. The Goosebumps series of books contains many titles about ghosts and spirits.

GHOSTS ON FILM

Ghosts have been popular film subjects since the beginning of motion pictures. Films were based on books with ghostly characters. Two examples are the comedies *Topper* in 1937 and *The Ghost and Mrs. Muir* in 1947. Both of these films were the basis of later television shows.

Ghost films took a dark turn with *The Haunting* in 1963, *The Legend of Hell House* in 1973, *The Shining* in 1980, and *Poltergeist* in 1982. These movies combined haunted houses with horror, terrifying viewers with suspense and violence.

Ghost-themed comedies returned in the 1980s. Both *Ghostbusters* in 1984 and *Beetlejuice* in 1988 sparked cartoon TV series. *Field of Dreams* in 1989 featured ghostly baseball players. *Ghost* in 1990 was a romantic thriller in which the spirit of a murdered man saves his wife from murder. *The Sixth Sense*, a thriller about a young boy who can see ghosts, was a hit in 1999. *The Woman in Black* in 2012 and *The Conjuring* in 2013 are two more recent paranormal films.

The old miser Ebenezer Scrooge is visited by the ghost of his greedy partner, Jacob Marley, who is cursed to wander the earth in chains.

GHOSTS ON TELEVISION

Ghosts have long been a popular topic for television shows. The animated *Casper the Friendly Ghost* charmed children in the 1940s. It even became a comic book series. *Scooby-Doo, Where are You?*, starring a large Great Dane and his human ghost-hunting friends, arrived on TV in the late 1960s. *Are You Afraid of the Dark?* aired in the 1990s on Nickelodeon. Some of the scary stories in each episode featured ghosts.

Ghost-hunting reality shows became popular after the hit movie *Ghostbusters* was released. One

GHOST DOG

Some people believe that animals can come back from the dead as ghosts. According to author Brad Steiger, in 1916, a retired Scotland Yard inspector took a photograph of a family having tea. A dog, which was not present at the event, appeared in the photo. There are stories about ghostly cats as well. Workers at the Capitol, in Washington, D.C., say that an evil cat haunts the basement's halls and tunnels. There is a legend that seeing the cat means that something bad will happen.

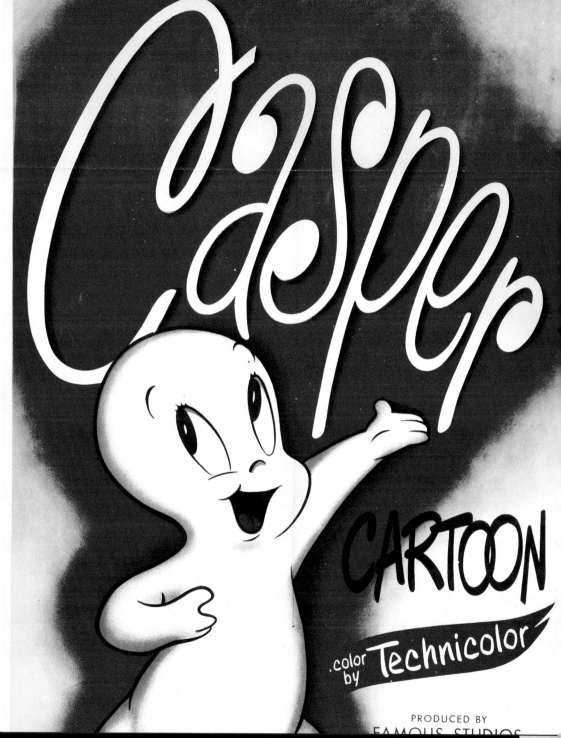

The original Casper the Friendly Ghost preferred the company of people instead of the community of ghosts who inhabited a haunted house.

of the earliest was *Ghost Hunters*. This show, which began in 2004 on the Sci Fi (now Syfy) Channel, featured two former plumbers investigating places that were said to be haunted. Ghost-hunting reality shows have appeared on such networks as Fox, Discovery, and the History Channel. The Travel Channel show *Ghost Adventures* explores haunted places all over the world. There is even a show on Animal Planet called *The Haunted* that features ghost investigations involving animals.

Investigators in the reality series Ghost Hunters *record thousands of hours of audio and video, looking for evidence of paranormal activity.*

SMARTPHONE AND TABLET APPS

Ghost hunters can find fun and useful smartphone and tablet applications. There are EMF detectors and EVP recorder apps for smartphones. For instance, *Ghost Radar* claims to sense ghosts in the area by reading energy fields, and spirits can allegedly even choose words from a database to communicate with the ghost hunter.

GHOST GAMES

It is not surprising that ghosts have become a topic for games. Casper the Friendly Ghost became a board game in 1959. Green Ghost, produced in 1965, was the first board game created for playing in the dark. Other ghostly board games include Haunted House, Ghost, Betrayal at House on the Hill, and Goosebumps: Terror in the Graveyard.

Ghosts have also made their way into video games, beginning with the *Pac-Man* arcade game in 1980. Casper and the Ghostbusters team have their own games. The game *Luigi's Mansion* is part of the Mario franchise. In it a character captures ghosts with the Poltergeist 3000, a vacuum cleaner. Other ghost and haunted house games

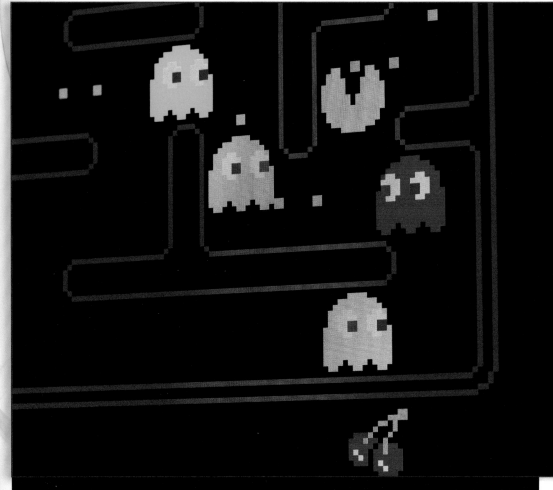

The popular arcade and video game Pac-Man *uses the four ghost characters to provide interest and difficulty for game players.*

are *Haunt* (Xbox 360), *Ghost Trick: Phantom Detective* (Nintendo DS), the *Blackwell* series (Microsoft Windows), and *Cursed Mountain* (Wii).

Ghosts can be an exciting topic to explore. Some people see and hear things they can't explain.

Other people are curious about what happens to them after death. Many people just enjoy being scared by a good ghost story or a haunted house. No one knows if ghosts really exist. Ghost investigators stress that it is important to use good critical-thinking skills and to always look for real evidence. Both skeptics and believers agree that learning about ghosts can be an amazing experience.

GLOSSARY

APPARITION An unusual or unexpected sight.

CARBON MONOXIDE A colorless, odorless, poisonous gas formed by the incomplete burning of carbon.

CRITICAL THINKING Analysis and evaluation through reasoning.

DEDUCE To determine by reasoning from a general rule or principle.

DORMANT Not active but capable of becoming active.

ELECTROMAGNET A natural force arising from interactions between charged particles.

ELIZABETHAN Of, relating to, or suggesting Elizabeth I of England or her time from 1558–1603.

EXORCISE To drive evil spirits out of a person.

FORMALDEHYDE A colorless gas that consists of carbon, hydrogen, and oxygen; has a sharp irritating odor; and when dissolved in water is used to disinfect or to prevent decay.

FREQUENCY The number of waves (as of sound or electromagnetic energy) that pass a fixed point each second.

GEIGER COUNTER An instrument for detecting the presence of radioactive substances.

HALLUCINATION The awareness of something (as a visual image, a sound, or a smell) that seems to be experienced through one of the senses but is not real and cannot be sensed by someone else.

HIEROGLYPHICS An ancient Egyptian system of writing mainly in pictorial characters.

INFRASOUND Sound that is lower in frequency than the "normal" limit of human hearing.

MEDIUM A person who acts as a go-between for people and spirits.

METHANE A colorless, odorless, flammable gas that consists of carbon and hydrogen and is produced by decay of organic matter.

ORB Something in the shape of a ball.

PARANORMAL Outside the range of normal experience or scientific explanation.

PAUPER A very poor person, sometimes supported by charity.

POLTERGEIST A mischievous ghost thought to be the cause of mysterious noises and actions.

RITE An act used in a religious ceremony.

SÉANCE A meeting to receive the communications of spirits.

SEISMOGRAPH A device to measure and record vibrations of the earth.

SKEPTICAL Relating to or marked by doubt.

SPIRITUALISM A belief that the spirits of the dead communicate with the living.

SUBCONSCIOUS Existing in the mind but not immediately available to consciousness.

SUPERNATURAL Above or beyond what is natural; unexplainable by natural law.

THERAPIST A person trained to use psychological methods to overcome mental health problems..

TRANCE A half-conscious state between sleeping and waking.

FOR FURTHER READING

BOOKS

Belanger, Jeff. *Ghosts of War*. (Haunted: Ghosts and the Paranormal). New York, NY: Rosen Publishing Group, 2009.

Belanger, Jeff. *Paranormal Encounters* (Haunted: Ghosts and the Paranormal). New York, NY: Rosen Publishing Group, 2012.

Belanger, Jeff. *Real-Life Ghost Encounters*. (Haunted: Ghosts and the Paranormal). New York, NY: Rosen Publishing Group, 2013.

Belanger, Jeff. *Who's Haunting the White House?* New York: NY: Sterling Publishing Co., Inc., 2008.

Belanger, Jeff. *World's Most Haunted Places*. (Haunted: Ghosts and the Paranormal). New York, NY: Rosen Publishing Group, 2009.

Curran, Bob. *The Scariest Places in the World*. (Haunted: Ghosts and the Paranormal). New York, NY: Rosen Publishing Group, 2013.

Hall, William. *The World's Most Haunted House*. Pompton Plains, NJ: The Career Press, 2014.

Haughton, Brian. *Famous Ghost Stories*. (Haunted: Ghosts and the Paranormal). New York, NY: Rosen Publishing Group, 2012.

Hawes, Jason, and Grant Wilson. *Ghost Files*. New York, NY: Gallery Books, 2011.

Jones, Marie D. *Modern Science and the Paranormal*. (Haunted: Ghosts and the Paranormal). New York, NY: Rosen Publishing Group, 2009.

Osborne, Mary Pope, and Natalie Pope Boyce. *Ghosts* (Magic Tree House Research Guide). New York, NY: Random House, 2009.

Shores, Lori. *Ghosts: Truth and Rumors*. Mankato, MN: Capstone Press, 2010.

Webb, Stuart. *Ghosts* (Paranormal Files). New York, NY: Rosen Publishing Group, 2013.

WEBSITES

Because of the changing nature of Internet links, Rosen Publishing has developed an online list of websites related to the subject of this book. This site is updated regularly. Please use this link to access this list:

http://www.rosenlinks.com/UTP/Ghost

INDEX